The Joy of the Gospel

A Companion Guide
to *Evangelii Gaudium*

by
Petroc Willey & Barbara Davies

*All booklets are published thanks to the
generous support of the members of the
Catholic Truth Society*

CATHOLIC TRUTH SOCIETY
PUBLISHERS TO THE HOLY SEE

Contents

ISBN 978 1 78469 022 9

Foreword

When I asked Petroc Willey and Barbara Davies to produce a guided reading of *The Joy of the Gospel*, I had in mind the enabling of as many people as possible to benefit from the teaching and encouragement offered in Pope Francis's Apostolic Exhortation. The Holy Father's letter is so full of the ardour needed for a new evangelisation.

Whether it be used for personal reading or together with others, I am sure this guide will be of great assistance to those wishing to enter into Pope Francis's vision. Bringing out its profoundly Marian character, it shows its roots both in the Second Vatican Council and in the teaching of his immediate predecessors.

I highly recommend this Companion Guide. My hope is that it will inspire you to become more faithfully a "missionary disciple" under the guidance of Pope Francis and his chosen patron, Saint Francis of Assisi.

+ Mark
Bishop of Shrewsbury

Introduction

In 1975, Pope Paul VI wrote his Apostolic Exhortation, *Joy in The Lord (Gaudete in Domino)*. In this, he explored the Beatitudes and the meaning of *real* Christian joy, as opposed to the illusory pleasures which are so often sought to fill the gap that can only be satisfied by the joy which Christ brings. It is to this work of Paul VI that Pope Francis turns first of all, in his own new and beautiful exhortation for all God's people, *The Joy of the Gospel (Evangelii Gaudium)*.

These two works have much in common. Both are, for example, profoundly Marian in character. Paul VI turns to Mary as the one who, summing up in herself God's intentions for all his people, is also the one filled with perfect joy. "With Christ," he says, "[Mary] sums up in herself all joys; she lives the perfect joy promised to the Church: *Mater plena sanctae laetitiae*. And it is with good reason that her children on earth, turning to her who is the mother of hope and of grace, invoke her as the cause of their joy: *Causa nostrae laetitiae*." Pope Francis also leads us towards a final contemplation of Mary as "the friend who is ever concerned that wine be not lacking in our lives", and who, as the "Mother of the Church which evangelises", shows each of us how to "bring forth Christ".

Paul VI and Francis also emphasise that Mary, who lives perfect Christian joy, points the way to what Pope Paul describes as the "humble and joyous service of the disinherited and of those on the margins of society. For joy cannot be dissociated from sharing. In God himself, all is joy because all is giving". Pope Francis concurs: in Mary, we see the one who "sets out from her town 'with haste' to be of service to others".

The joy which belongs to Mary because she is full of God's grace, is the same joy which Pope Francis, like his predecessor, wants each person to experience today. What is more, he emphasises that this joy is within our reach. It is, in fact, offered freely to us by the Lord himself, who wants nothing more than to help us into the loving arms of his Father, the ultimate source and origin of all life and all joy.

The focus of Pope Francis's Exhortation is on the proclamation of the Gospel in the world of today. He wants to show us how joy, flowing from an encounter with the Lord, can "give shape to a definite style of evangelisation" and have an effect upon every action we undertake. This booklet is intended to assist us in appreciating all of the ways indicated by Pope Francis.

Features of the Guide

This Guide is intended merely to accompany the reading of *Evangelii Gaudium*. It can be read on one's own, or it can be used in small groups. It is important to realise that the Guide does not replace the text of *Evangelii Gaudium*, but rather sits alongside it. It leads into a direct reading of the Pope's text, rather than providing a summary of it. The introduction to *Evangelii Gaudium* presents us with the themes of the whole text. Because of this, the Guide focuses on this introduction, and shows how the Exhortation teases out what is evoked there throughout the other chapters.

This Guide to *Evangelii Gaudium* is set out carefully so that you pray with Pope Francis's text, meditating upon its meaning in the light of the Scriptures and of some of the sources from Tradition which have provided the Pope - and can provide us - with inspiration.

The meditative approach taken here is also intended to facilitate an encounter with Christ so that we are responsive to his call to ongoing conversion. Every page of *Evangelii Gaudium* emphasises Christ's call to each of the baptised to a deeper reception of his love, and to a renewed self-examination for the sake of mission.

Each chapter begins with Scripture; it includes a longer text which reflects the same theme of the Exhortation. Scripture is always to be the "soul" of our work, says Pope Francis (see, for example, *EG* 174-5). Scripture is not to be used simply as a "proof-text" for what we have decided for other reasons, but as the genuine driving force of our thinking and living.

The Guide also reflects the fact that the liturgy is the "source and summit" of the faith, such that the Church's teaching is always reflected in her prayer; it flows from, and leads back to liturgy (*EG* 24). A simple liturgical approach is used: there is an opening phrase, usually from a Psalm, a recitation of either the *Benedictus* or the *Magnificat*, and a closing *Collect*.

The Guide highlights the sources used by *Evangelii Gaudium*. As a work of the teaching office of the Church (the papal 'magisterium'), Pope Francis's Exhortation is rooted in the riches of both Scripture and Tradition. Like all such documents, it serves the Word of God who is transmitted in and through the living sources of the faith. The Guide expresses this through short references to the lives of the saints, to other papal teaching, and to the *Catechism*. This approach allows us to appreciate what Pope Francis calls the "eternal newness" of Christ, which is given new expression in every stage of the Church's life and shines through the Pope's ardour.

Finally, the Guide helps us to be practical. It links the Exhortation to daily life in three ways: through a simple reflection on short readings from the document; through an appreciation of how the teaching in *Evangelii Gaudium* is illustrated by the life of St Francis of Assisi, Pope Francis's namesake; and through questions for reflection, which allow a more considered and extended response to the Pope's ideas.

The Chapters

Chapter 1: The Joy of the Gospel. The Guide begins by introducing the theme of the entire work - joy - and the importance of promoting an encounter with Christ.

Chapter 2: The Joy of the Poor in Spirit. The Guide presents the call to be a humble, poor Church, living out the Beatitudes and depending on the grace of God which Pope Francis reiterates in every section of the Exhortation.

Chapter 3: The Joy of Conversion. The central theme of the first chapter of *Evangelii Gaudium* is the need for the Church to undergo a radical, ongoing conversion for the sake of mission.

Chapter 4: The Joy of Life Together in Christ. The Pope sees the main challenge we face today as a "crisis of communal commitment". This so often characterises relationships in the world and even influences relationships in the Church, as the Pope shows in Chapter Two.

Chapter 5: The Joy of the Herald. The Exhortation's major theme is the need to proclaim the Gospel. Pope Francis makes this the key focus of the central section of *Evangelii Gaudium*, his Chapter Three.

Chapter 6: The Joy of Those Who Love the Poor Christ.
The joy of reaching out to the poor and the excluded is
developed in Chapter Four of *Evangelii Gaudium*.

**Chapter 7: The Joy of Mary, Star of the New
Evangelisation.** In the final chapter of *Evangelii Gaudium*,
Mary is held up to us as the one who shows us how to be
"Spirit-filled evangelisers".

The Structure of each Chapter of the Guide

A theme heading sets out the topic for reflection.

Each chapter begins with Scripture and prayer. The
Scripture is usually reflective of the liturgy of the Easter
season, expressing joy. This is followed by the prayer of
the *Benedictus* - except in the final chapter, when it is
the *Magnificat* (both texts are provided at the end of the
Guide). Each chapter concludes with a short period of
meditation and prayer.

A brief introduction then explains the focus of the
particular reflection.

This is followed by a reading from the introduction
of *Evangelii Gaudium*, followed by a time of personal
reflection, or of sharing if one is in a group. Several related
paragraphs in the document are also suggested for close
attention. To facilitate the reading of the entire document
various schema are presented at the end of the Guide.

Three elements are then introduced, to deepen an understanding of Pope Francis's text:

• A portion of Scripture central to the theme.

• A short passage relating the theme from *Evangelii Gaudium* to the life of St Francis, the saint who is the particular inspiration for Pope Francis himself, as an illustrative example of Christian living and wisdom.

• Brief explanatory notes on the passage from *Evangelii Gaudium*.

The chapter then moves into a period for either personal reflection or group discussion; suggested tasks and questions allow for a deepening of one's understanding of the topic and for an application in one's daily life.

The conclusion consists of a prayerful reading of a summary paragraph on the same theme taken from the *Catechism of the Catholic Church*, the recitation of the *Our Father* and a final prayer.

Prelude: The Annunciation

At the end of *The Gospel of Joy*, Pope Francis turns to
Our Lady in prayer:

Mary, Virgin and Mother,
you who, moved by the Holy Spirit,
welcomed the word of life
in the depths of your humble faith:
as you gave yourself completely to the Eternal One,
help us to say our own "yes"
to the urgent call, as pressing as ever,
to proclaim the good news of Jesus.

The work of our salvation depended upon the "yes" of
this poor maiden of Nazareth. Her receiving of the Word
of Life, in a trusting handing-over of herself to God, is the
model for each member of the Church. For we too, in our
place and time, are called to receive Christ and to manifest
his loving-kindness to our world.

The setting in the painting of the Annunciation, by
Ossawa Tanner,[1] is strikingly realistic. It portrays a poor
stone house in Nazareth; a typical country rug lies on the
floor; there's a lamp, three jars and little else.

The intense point of interest which immediately holds our attention is Mary's enquiring look towards the bright light which depicts the angelic being. This is the pure spirit, the Archangel Gabriel. Mary's disposition recalls St Luke's account of the Annunciation *(Lk* 1:26-38). Is this the moment when Mary "pondered what this greeting could mean", or when she asks, "How can this be, for I am a virgin"?

We notice, too, that Mary is sitting in a posture of respectful listening before the angel, just as another Mary who, in the Gospel, sat at the feet of Christ, having chosen "the one thing necessary" *(Lk* 10:39). Hands clasped firmly together, Mary seems to be searching all she knows and believes of God's wonders for her people in history, while Gabriel tells her that the Child to be born of her will have the throne of his father, David, and he will rule "over the House of Jacob for ever".

A closer look at the hues Tanner uses allows the delicate symbolism to emerge: the blueness of the cloak reminds us that this is the colour associated with Our Lady - blue, because she is full of heavenly grace; the resplendent white of the linen is suggestive of the fact that this young woman is a virgin and utterly pure; and the red backcloth calls to mind the crucifixion of the Child about to be conceived. Rivers of unbleached cloth, flowing all around the seated figure of Mary, on the blanket and in her own gown, gush out onto the floor: it is as if the mystery of who Our Lady is in the plan of God and what she has just heard of its fulfilment, cannot be contained. They also tell us that the answer this girl gives will, like a stone cast in the stream of time, have a ripple effect for ever.

The simplicity of the poor in spirit, the joy of the angelic message, the mystery of grace transforming the most ordinary of settings, and the costly love of the work of our redemption - such are the great themes portrayed in Tanner's picture, the same which lie at the heart of *Evangelii Gaudium* to which we now turn.

Chapter 1: The Joy of the Gospel

The Lord brought out his people with joy,
his chosen ones with shouts of rejoicing, alleluia!
(Ps 104:43)

"Rejoice in the Lord always; again I say, Rejoice!"
(Ph 4:4) The Christian life is characterised by joy.
This simple truth is what Pope Francis wants to
present to us in his new letter to the Church. He has
called his message: *The Joy of the Gospel* - in its
Latin title, *Evangelii Gaudium.*[2] In this Guide, we
will be praying with, and seeking to learn from, Pope
Francis's encouraging message. What a wonderful
opportunity this is for us to deepen our awareness of
how the Lord fills our lives with his joy!

We pray *The Benedictus*

The importance of joy was also a key theme for Pope Benedict,
whom Pope Francis cites many times in the document we are
reading. Our joy comes from the fact that Jesus Christ, our
Lord and God, has invited us to be his friends:

There is nothing more beautiful than to know Christ and
to speak to others of our friendship with him. The task

of the shepherd…can often seem wearisome. But it is beautiful and wonderful, because it is truly a service to joy, to God's joy which longs to break into the world.[3]

Like Pope Benedict, Pope Francis wants to ensure that we never forget this joy. He wants us to remind ourselves of its importance every single day so that it shapes our whole existence.

We read the text

In each session, we read a short portion from the introduction to *Evangelii Gaudium*, the summary of the entire work. We then explore how each portion is developed in the different chapters of the document. It is hoped that this reading and discussion will provide the inspiration for you to read the whole text in your own time.

We begin by reading the title page, the main chapter headings from the contents pages, and then the short opening paragraph, no. 1.[4]

Pause now to reflect and note something from what you have read, a specific phrase or sentence, that strikes you as important and which you would like to highlight.

In this first chapter, there are some introductory remarks we can make to help us to understand better what Pope Francis is communicating to us.

First of all, the document is an "*apostolic exhortation*" addressed to the Church:

• It is *apostolic*: this is because it is written by one who is a successor of the Apostles. Pope Francis is the successor of St Peter, who was appointed by Jesus to lead the Apostles;

• It is an *exhortation*: this characterises the style of the document. Francis *exhorts* us; he *appeals* to us; he seeks to motivate and move us to a renewed commitment and enthusiasm;

• It is *addressed to the Church*: unlike many papal writings which are addressed to "all men and women of good will", this is explicitly for the baptised - a point Pope Francis stresses many times in the document. The message given here is for all those who have already heard Christ's call and are seeking to hear his voice more clearly; we desire to learn better what it means to be united with Christ in love, to follow him, and to witness to him before others.

Secondly, *Evangelii Gaudium has been written in order to encourage us to proclaim the faith to those around us*. This is not a teaching document explaining the *content* of the faith, which is simply: God, and the revelation he makes to us in Jesus Christ, his Son, through the Holy Spirit, in and through the Church. Jesus himself is the joyful News we proclaim. In Christ we find the happiness and truth all people seek. Quoting from the

Scriptures, Pope Francis reminds us that "Christ is the 'eternal Gospel'…he is 'the same yesterday and today and forever'" (no. 11).

In our own day, the content of the faith has been explained and expressed with authority in the *Catechism of the Catholic Church*. Pope Francis refers us to this, and to other teaching documents of the Church; he encourages us to read widely, for we must know the truths of the faith which we are handing on.[5] He has written *Evangelii Gaudium* as a powerful appeal to us to take seriously *our part* in proclaiming the faith to others. Pope Francis wants to encourage a "renewed missionary impulse" (no. 262). He writes, "Here I have chosen to present some guidelines which can encourage and guide the whole Church in a new phase of evangelisation" (no. 17).

We learn from the Scriptures

In *Evangelii Gaudium* (no. 175), Pope Francis tells us that "evangelisation demands familiarity with God's word". He wants us to grasp the importance of studying Scripture. Quoting from Pope Benedict, he reminds us: "We do not blindly seek God, or wait for him to speak to us first, for 'God has already spoken, and there is nothing further that we need to know, which has not been revealed to us'". We will be turning to the Scriptures to receive the teaching of the eternal Son who came to show us the path to everlasting joy.

The centre of Jesus's teaching in the Gospels about the new life of joy he came to bring is called "The Beatitudes". 'Beatitude'[6] is a word that means 'happiness', but not just any kind of happiness. Jesus is speaking of a *divine* happiness, a happiness rooted in holiness. St Matthew records Jesus calling his disciples to him and describing for them the way to this true happiness.

Read: Matthew 5:1-12

The description we find in these verses is not the usual way in which the path to happiness is presented. To be poor in spirit, to mourn, to be meek, pure in heart, persecuted - these are not the first things that spring to mind when we want to describe how to live a happy life. Yet the Lord has told us that this *is* the way. What did he mean? How can we understand and explain this?

The Beatitudes describe a future state - they speak of the life of heaven to which Jesus is calling us. They remind us of the eternal joy to which we are called, which we will share for ever with God, Father, Son and Holy Spirit, with the angels and with all of the friends of God (see no. 267). St Paul warns us not to try to imagine heaven. He says it is "What no eye has seen, no ear heard, nor the heart of man conceived", but rather "what God has prepared for those who love him" (*1 Co* 2:9). The glories we perceive through sight, hearing and the senses in general, can only hint at what awaits us.

And yet, we *can* share in something of the happiness of heaven even now. Heaven is life with Christ, the one who loves us without reserve; and he is with us here and now, even in the darkness, uncertainties and difficulties of this life (see no. 266). He already stands with us as our friend, our comforter and redeemer. The very conditions of which the Beatitudes speak - poverty, being pure in heart, mourning, meekness, being persecuted when we do right - can even be welcomed, once we realise that Jesus is allowing us to share in his life. He is close to us and sustains us in these experiences, however painful they may be. "I understand the grief of people who have to endure great suffering", Pope Francis says. "Yet slowly but surely we all have to let the joy of faith slowly revive as a quiet yet firm trust" (no. 6).

We learn from St Francis

Pope Francis chose his name in honour of this twelfth-century Italian saint who founded the Franciscan order, someone who knew these things from experience, St Francis of Assisi. Pope Francis especially wants us to learn from the simplicity and poverty of St Francis and from St Francis's willingness to share the sufferings of others. In this Guide we shall therefore look back to the example of this great saint, and to stories from his life which link to *Evangelii Gaudium*.

Let us begin with a remarkable account. One of the early disciples of St Francis, Brother Leo, asks St Francis what perfect joy is. The saint, in answer, asks Brother Leo to imagine the following: "We have arrived at a convent, seeking shelter, drenched with rain and trembling with cold, covered with mud and exhausted from hunger. We knock at the convent-gate, but the porter comes out angrily to ask us who we are. We tell him that we are two of the friars, but he doesn't believe us. 'You are just impostors taking away the alms of the poor!' He refuses to open the door to us to us, leaving us outside, exposed to the snow and rain, suffering from cold and hunger." St Francis then adds, "If we accept such injustice, such cruelty and such contempt without being ruffled and without murmuring; if we bear all these injuries with patience and joy, thinking of the sufferings of our Blessed Lord, which we are sharing out of love for him - then here Brother Leo, is perfect joy."

Only love can understand this story! Think of someone you love very deeply - a spouse, a child, a parent, a dear friend... We *can* understand the sentiment St Francis expresses because this *is* how we feel about the ones we truly love: we want to share in their lives, we want to understand them; and when we see them suffering, we would gladly take their suffering upon ourselves, to be with them in their pain. Because of his great love for the Lord, at the end of his life St Francis was granted the gift of the *stigmata*, receiving the five wounds of Christ in his body. Pope Francis writes at the end of the Exhortation of the temptation to "keep the Lord's wounds at arm's length". He invites us instead to unite ourselves to the "suffering flesh of others" (no. 270).

The story about perfect joy seems surprising and even extreme, just as the Beatitudes of Jesus are not what we expect. Yet the point is simple: St Francis wants us to realise that nothing is of any importance besides the joy of being loved by the Lord, of loving him in return, and lovingly identifying with Christ. St Paul said: "I count everything as loss because of the surpassing worth of knowing Christ Jesus my Lord" (*Ph* 3:8).

We reflect

Let us read the next two paragraphs from Pope Francis's Apostolic Exhortation, *The Joy of the Gospel*.

Read: Evangelii Gaudium nos. 2-3

Questions for reflection

1. In no. 2, Pope Francis writes about what endangers Christian joy. Are there phrases he uses that particularly speak to you from your own experience?

2. In no. 3, Pope Francis writes about lasting joy. Notice the times he uses the phrase "once more". Why does he repeat this phrase so often? And why do you think he speaks of coming to Jesus as taking a "risk"? What is being risked?

3. Each Christian is called by God to a joyful future, and ultimately to everlasting joy, a sharing in the happiness

of the love of the Trinity (see nos. 111, 117, 178, 283). Recall one occasion when you experienced the happiness of the Christian faith, whether as a child, an adolescent or as an adult, when you knew that God is real, that he loves you.

4. Identify one aspect about the Christian faith that you want others to know because it brings happiness.

Meditation and final prayer

As we conclude, we turn to the Lord. First, let us read prayerfully *CCC* 1720-1721.

Pause for silent reflection

We pray the *Our Father*

May your people exult for ever, O God,
in renewed youthfulness of spirit,
So that, rejoicing now in the restored glory of
our adoption,
we may look forward in confident hope
to the rejoicing of the day of resurrection.
Through our Lord Jesus Christ, your Son,
who lives and reigns with you in the unity of
the Holy Spirit,
one God, for ever and ever. Amen.

(Collect from Third Sunday of Easter)

Chapter 2: The Joy of the Poor in Spirit

"Blessed are the poor in spirit,
for theirs is the kingdom of Heaven"
(*Mt* 5:3).

In the last chapter we read the opening pages from Pope Francis's *The Joy of the Gospel*. We remembered the Lord's own promise of the perfect joy that awaits us, and which we can already begin to enjoy - the blessings of heaven which Jesus calls 'Beatitudes'. Let us read another section from Pope Francis's message on joy as he focuses our attention on the Scriptures and the solid foundation of all Christian joy - the state which Jesus describes as being "poor in spirit".

We pray *The Benedictus*

We read the text

We continue our discovery of *Evangelii Gaudium* as we read nos. 4-5. These two paragraphs draw our attention to the importance of the theme of joy in the Old Testament (no. 4) and in the New Testament (no. 5).

Pause now to reflect and note something from what you have read, a specific phrase or sentence, that strikes you as important and which you would like to highlight.

To be poor in spirit means to know our need for God. It means to know that we depend upon him for everything. In the words of St Augustine, it means to be a "beggar before God". Beggars ask for what they need, and Jesus reassures us, "Ask, and it will be given you" (*Mt* 7:7). This is the way Jesus lived with regard to his Father, the eternal Son being filled with the love of his Father; it was the deepest source of his joy. Pope Francis reminds us that Jesus wants us to share in this same joy, this same relationship with the Father, the joy of the poor in spirit: "I have said these things to you, so that my joy may be in you and that your joy may be complete" (*Jn* 15:11).

In order to help us understand this Christian joy of being "poor in spirit", of being a beggar before God, Pope Francis points us to a vivid image from the prophet Zechariah. The prophet invites the people of Israel to rejoice when they see the great example of the *humility of their King*, "humble and riding on a donkey".

It is a powerful reference, fulfilled by Jesus himself when he entered into Jerusalem at the beginning of his Passion. Jesus, the eternal Son, is teaching us by his own life how to depend upon the Father for all things. He is King, but does not seize his rightful Kingdom by force. He follows a different way, entrusting his life to the Father.

This moment is remembered at each celebration of the Mass when we, the People of God, rejoice, singing the *Sanctus* (see *Lk* 19:28-40). At Mass we are invited to be part of the great drama of the humility of the King who lives the way of trust in the Father and of love for us "to the end" (*Jn* 13:1).

Pope Francis then draws our attention to the prophet Zephaniah, to a passage which he describes as "thrilling to reread". It is the description of the Lord himself who is full of joy because of his great love for us! The Pope continues, "This is the joy which we experience daily". He then quotes from the Wisdom literature, reminding us not to deprive ourselves of the day's enjoyment. We must be poor in spirit, remembering that we can ask our Father whose joy it is to give us all we need. The Father cares for us even "amid the little things of life". Let's not deprive ourselves of the joy God takes in us!

We have the happiness of heaven to which we can look forward. The joy that Christ gives us is not only in the future, however; it is available for us day by day. This truth is beautifully expressed in Alice Meynell's poem, "I am the Way".

> Thou art the Way.
> Hadst Thou been nothing but the goal,
> I cannot say
> If Thou hadst ever met my soul.

I cannot see -
I, child of process - if there lies
An end for me,
Full of repose, full of replies.

I'll not reproach
The road that winds, my feet that err.
Access, Approach
Art thou, Time, Way, and Wayfarer.

We learn from the Scriptures

Pope Francis has been helping us to see that the joy of the Gospel is not just our joy but, more deeply, the joy that belongs uniquely to *God the Blessed Trinity*. The joy of the Gospel is the joy of our heavenly Father, the joy of the eternal Son, the joy of the Holy Spirit. Our joy is found when we learn to receive and appreciate the over-flowing joyous love of the Blessed Trinity for each one of us (see nos. 111, 117, 178, 283).

Let us turn to a famous passage from the Scriptures which expresses the truth that God the Son gave everything so that we might become rich with this same joy. The Son humbled himself, became a beggar, so that he might become the joyful Way for us in each moment. He invites us to learn with him that the path to heaven lies in being poor in spirit. Then we can experience the riches of the love the Father wants to give us here and now, and after death be rich in the life of heaven (see also *2 Co* 8:9).

Read: Philippians 2:5-11

Pope Francis quotes from this passage later in *Evangelii Gaudium* (cf. no. 198), reminding us to "put on the mind of Christ", as St Paul teaches. Sharing in the mind of Christ, we come to see that Christian joy is not a surface pleasure or superficial experience of happiness. It is a sharing in the life of the Blessed Trinity. It does not avoid the sacrifice asked of all who love, but grows and develops more deeply from such sacrifice. Pope Francis puts it like this: "The Gospel, radiant with the glory of Christ's cross, constantly invites us to rejoice" (no. 5).

We learn from St Francis

We turn now to learn from St Francis. The path of Christian joy followed by each of the Church's saints is associated in our minds with some particular virtue, apostolate, or unique spiritual approach. For instance, St John Chrysostom is especially remembered for his eloquent preaching; St Thérèse of Lisieux for her "Little Way", and St Maria Goretti for her exemplary purity.

St Francis's particular path to joy lay in his devotion to poverty. St Francis, one of the great inspirations of Pope Francis after Jesus Christ, considered himself "married" to the one he liked to call his "Lady Poverty". When asked by his followers which virtue draws one closest to Christ, he helped them to understand that poverty is the special way to salvation, for "it is the food of humility, and the root of perfection". St Bonaventure commented: "No one was ever so covetous after gold as Francis of poverty."

His striving after perfect poverty was motivated by two things: a trust in Divine Providence, in the utterly reliable love of the Father who would care for him; and a desire to unite himself to Christ more perfectly. He saw poverty as "the ever-familiar and beloved companion of the Son of God". One of the early stories about St Francis illustrates these two points. Following the Rule of the Order, Francis and another friar, Brother Masseo, were begging for their food. St Francis took one street, and Brother Masseo the other. The account records that St Francis, being a "little man, with a mean exterior", attracted little attention, and he gathered only a few bits of dry bread, whereas Brother Masseo, being "tall and good-looking", received several whole loaves.

When they had ended their task, they met on a spot outside the city where there was a beautiful fountain, and a large stone on which each placed what he had collected. St Francis was overjoyed: "O Brother Masseo, we are not worthy of this great treasure". Brother Masseo, sceptical, answered: "How can you talk of a 'treasure'? We have no knife, no dish, no table, no house to eat in, no servant or maid to wait upon us." St Francis answered: "This is the reason *why* I call it a great treasure - because everything we have has been given to us by Divine Providence, as we can clearly see in this bread of charity, this beautiful table of stone, and this clear fountain. So let us beg God to make us love with all our hearts the treasure of holy poverty."

We reflect

We have seen that poverty is the special legacy St Francis has left to the Orders he founded. He asked that his followers live the most primitive of lifestyles and rely totally upon Divine Providence for all their needs.

The majority of Catholics cannot imitate literally the kind of poverty that St Francis sought with such zeal. Pope Francis wants us, nonetheless, to take seriously in our own life the call to have a spirit of detachment so that we can practise a real reliance upon Divine Providence. He wants us to learn the secret of the joy of being poor in spirit, to have the confidence of children who know they have a heavenly Father who wants them to look to him and to his love as their daily source of joy.

Questions for reflection

1. What in today's session has helped you to appreciate more deeply the joy of being poor in spirit?

2. When has mercy and generosity been shown to you by another when you were poor (materially, or otherwise in need)? What have you understood about the blessings of poverty from this experience?

3. Notice the repetition of the words "invite" and "invitation" in the paragraphs we have been reading. How does the use of such terms highlight our dignity before God and the Lord's deep respect for us?

4. To what kinds of need around you might the Lord be calling you to respond?

Meditation and final prayer

As we conclude, we turn to the Lord. First, let us read prayerfully *CCC* 2546-2547.

Pause for silent reflection

We pray the *Our Father*

O God, by whose gift St Francis
Was conformed to Christ in poverty and humility,
Grant that, by walking in Francis's footsteps,
We may follow your Son,
And, through joyful charity, come to be united
with you.
Through our Lord Jesus Christ, your Son,
who lives and reigns with you in the unity of
the Holy Spirit,
one God, for ever and ever. Amen.

(Collect from the Memorial of St Francis of Assisi)

Chapter 3: The Joy of Conversion

"I have gone astray like a lost sheep;
seek your servant for I do not forget your commands"
(*Ps* 118:176).

Pope Francis's message to us is a call to rediscover the joy that flows from the on-going conversion to Christ. The first and fundamental moment of conversion for every Christian is Baptism: this is where, in our own name or through others, we renounce sin and receive the gift of new life. The call to discover the joy that flows from turning from the selfishness of sin to a new and richer way of living is ongoing. We will see that conversion is described as an "uninterrupted task" for each member of Christ's Body.

We pray *The Benedictus*

We read the text

We continue our reading of *Evangelii Gaudium* with nos. 6-8. The focus of these paragraphs is friendship with Christ and how he leads us into a more deeply satisfying life, if we will only let him overcome the barriers we throw in his way.

Pause now to reflect and note something from what you have read, a specific phrase or sentence, that strikes you as important and which you would like to highlight.

At the start of his pontificate, every pope chooses a personal motto which is then written in Latin below his coat of arms. Pope Francis chose a phrase that can be translated either as "Lowly, yet chosen", or "To be pitied, yet chosen". Explaining his choice, Pope Francis recalls a powerful experience he had of God's mercy. It took place in 1953, on the Feast of St Matthew, during the Sacrament of Confession. As with the story of that saint in the Gospel, the young man, in a moment of grace, understood both God's forgiveness and his call: to be a Jesuit priest.

The paragraphs we have just read contain this double message of mercy and call. At the end of the section, Pope Francis writes: "For if we have received the love which restores meaning to our lives, how can we fail to share that love with others?" This is something so fundamental that it is very important we grasp Pope Francis's meaning. "Goodness", he says, "always tends to spread" (no. 9).

These are sentiments which echo the advice given by St Bernard of Clairvaux in an earlier century: "Learn to flow over", he said. Be filled first, and then flow out from this abundance towards others. Receive God's mercy in your own life; then show that mercy to others. Pope Francis, like St Bernard, longs for us to be able to draw upon our own experience of deep joy at the unconditional mercy of God.

Once we can recognise how the Lord works in our own lives, we will want to point others in the same direction.

In the paragraphs we have read, Pope Francis provides us with a three-point plan for our on-going conversion:

- *See your life from God's point of view*. The single essential element here is that "we are infinitely loved" (no. 6). Whatever else is true, and whatever kind of suffering or difficulties we are enduring, this remains the unshakeable bedrock.

- *Don't wait for life to change before you think happiness can be found*. Happiness is not so much about getting life to 'fit us', as to 'fit ourselves' to the deepest truth about life: namely, the reality of friendship with Christ (nos. 7 and 8).

- *Understand the difference between pleasure and joy* (no. 7). Pleasure has to do with the senses, with what we see, feel, touch. Technology provides answers which address many of the needs related to bodily comforts and pleasures, but mere pleasure is a far cry from joy. As embodied spirits who can think and choose and love, our joy is to be found not in feelings but in our relationship with Jesus Christ, a relationship which will last for ever. We find joy when we let God take us 'beyond ourselves'. This is the source both of true joy and of our witness to the Good News of friendship with Christ (no. 8). Since it has to do with the spiritual nature of our humanity, this joy is available to every human being - both to those who are technologically rich, and to "poor people who [have] little to hold on to".

We learn from the Scriptures

Pope Francis helps us to see that on-going conversion is not merely conversion away from sin; more truly, it is also an entry into a deeper and more satisfying life. This is the fundamental message of the Scriptures. In Revelation, the last book of the Bible, angels (meaning 'messengers from God') speak to the local Christian communities about the life of faith. Let us read the first of these messages:

Read: Rev 2:2-5

The Church the angel describes has many strengths: hard work, patience, endurance, resistance to evil, discernment. Its members can be proud of its achievements and steadfastness. Yet the community has abandoned the love of Christ which it had at its beginning. Without this love, the community is nothing (cf. *1 Co* 13:1-3).

How, then, is this love to be recovered? This cannot be by our own human strength. Pope Francis says that it comes only when we "let God" bring us to a new place. It is by his grace and through the gifts he pours out on us that we are renewed in our love for the Lord. Christ gives us the love with which we love him (*Rm* 5:5)! We can glimpse how this happens from the example of the life of Pope Francis's mentor, St Francis of Assisi.

We learn from St Francis

St Francis is a model of on-going Christian conversion. Like all the saints, he recognised the importance of always remaining completely open to the work of the Holy Spirit. He knew that God would need to change him over and again to make him an ever-more perfect instrument for the sanctification of others.

Francis was also a realist. He was aware of the all-too-human tendency to close off areas of life to God's healing work. He knew the many ways we find to keep God and others at a distance, to keep the heart's door closed rather than open (cf. no. 47). A major triumph was won soon after his conversion, thanks to his openness to the work of God's grace in his life. At great personal cost, Francis overcame his fear of leprosy by reverently kissing the hand of a leper who approached him for alms.

As Francis walked along the path of on-going conversion, his joy deepened. He knew the Lord calls everyone to the perfection of love, but that this could be expressed in many different ways. Few would follow St Francis in leaving behind family and possessions to strive after perfection as he had done. For others who were attracted to his spiritual path, he founded a 'Third Order' which any Christian could join. Francis wrote a 'Rule of Life' for them, guiding lay people in how to live as more deeply committed Christians in and through the ordinary responsibilities of daily life. This was the "Order of Penitents", and over the centuries has been a powerful vehicle for re-evangelisation, providing a practical framework for many men and women to grow in holiness.

We reflect

The central theme of Chapter One of *Evangelii Gaudium* (nos. 19-49) is, then, the need for the Church and all her members to take seriously the call to a radical, on-going conversion. Her mission to the world depends on her fidelity to this.

Pope Francis mentions various aspects of the Church's life, identifying obstacles to evangelisation: from the parish to all forms of associations, small or great; from the local Church with her bishop, to the universal Church and her bishop, the Pope himself. He invites everyone to be "bold and creative in the task of rethinking the goals, structures, style and method of evangelisation in their respective communities…without inhibitions or fear…especially under the leadership of the bishops, in a wise and realistic pastoral discernment" (no. 33).

The challenge is for every person to be truly evangelised first, and only then to obey the call to go out beyond one's "comfort zone" (no. 20). Time and again, Pope Francis draws attention to the double aspect of receiving-giving, the 'heart-beat' as it were of the Christian life:

• First be evangelised, then you will be able to go out and evangelise;

- Be renewed through the beauty of the liturgy, and draw others into it;

- Receive God's mercy, and show mercy to all;

- Receive Christ's love, then manifest this love to others;

- Understand the faith more deeply, and you will help others to do so.

In each case, the *sign* that we have received is that we, in turn, are willing to give. And the *condition* for our giving is that we ourselves know how to receive from the Lord.

There are many rich and challenging passages in this chapter. The following citations can provide us with a flavour of them:

- "An evangelising community knows that the Lord has taken the initiative, he has loved us first" (no. 24).

- "The disciple is ready to put his or her whole life on the line, even to accepting martyrdom, in bearing witness to Jesus Christ" (no. 24).

- "Christ summons the Church as she goes her pilgrim way... to that continual reformation of which she always has need, in so far as she is a human institution here on earth" (no. 26, quoting the Second Vatican Council).

- "The Church is called the house of the Father, its doors always wide open" (no. 47).

• "If something should rightly disturb us and trouble our consciences, it is the fact that so many of our brothers and sisters are living without the strength, light and consolation born of friendship with Jesus Christ, without a community of faith to support them, without meaning and a goal to life" (no. 49).

Questions for reflection

1. "I could only be happy, if…". Complete this sentence with something you care about. For example, "I could only be happy, if I had a good job"; "…if I were healthy"; "…if I had a regular holiday", etc.,. Now reflect on what you've said, and change it to something you've learnt from this chapter. For example: "I can only be happy if I am attentive to God's love for me/ if I trust God more/ if I learn to love God with all my heart…"

2. What are some of the specific areas in which you need to seek the Lord's renewing work so that you can communicate his truth, grace and love more fully?

3. What, from this chapter, has struck you as being important for the life of the parish/community/family to which you belong?

4. What examples can you think of, either from the Bible or from the lives of saints (perhaps your own patron) in which someone has experienced joy because of a 'change of heart'?

Meditation and final prayer

As we conclude, we turn to the Lord. First, let us read prayerfully *CCC* 1427-1429.

Pause for silent reflection

We pray the *Our Father*

O God, whose will it is that all should be saved
and come to the knowledge of the truth,
look upon your abundant harvest
and be pleased to send workers to gather it,
that the Gospel may be preached to all creation
and that your people, gathered by the word of life
and sustained by the power of the Sacraments,
may advance in the path of salvation and love.
Through our Lord Jesus Christ, your Son,
who lives and reigns with you in the unity of
the Holy Spirit,
One God, for ever and ever. Amen.

(Collect for the Evangelisation of Peoples)

Chapter 4: The Joy of Life Together in Christ

"A new commandment I give to you,
that you love one another;
even as I have loved you,
that you love one another" (*Jn* 13:34).

"The seventy-two returned with joy...Jesus rejoiced in the Holy Spirit, and said, 'I thank you Father!'" (*Lk* 10:17-21). Pope Francis ardently desires to enkindle in us the fire of this same *joy* for the Good News which the Father gave us in his Son through the Holy Spirit! The Pope repeatedly reminds us of the "newness" of what God has done for us. It is precisely because of this newness that the community of the Church is ever in need of renewal. We all need to be renewed, not merely as individuals but as the Church - the "people made one by the unity of the Father, the Son and the Spirit" (St Cyprian). St Paul reflects on this supernatural unity among Christians: "If one member suffers," he says, "all suffer together; if one member is honoured, all rejoice together" (*1 Co* 12:26). It is this joy of life together in Christ which is the theme for our reflection in this chapter.

We pray *The Benedictus*

We read the text

In his *Exhortation* (no. 17), Pope Francis tells us that, in proposing seven major themes, he is drawing on the teaching of one of Vatican II's principal documents, *Lumen Gentium*.[7] This is a very rich and beautiful text, one that as mature Catholics we should read for ourselves. It is good to bear in mind that *Evangelii Gaudium* is rooted in the teaching of the Second Vatican Council on "*the mystery of Christ and the Church*". Let us note, in passing, that there are not two mysteries here, only one.

The first of the Pope's themes, "The reform of the Church in her missionary outreach" is the topic of Chapter One of the Exhortation; we explored it in the first chapter of this Guide. Simply, it is this: for both the Fathers of Vatican II and for the Pope, the more true the Church is to the newness of life received in Christ, the more she will proclaim that life to the world so that all may share in an abundance of joy (no. 26).

This time, we are invited to focus on the fact that we rejoice not merely as individuals but as members of the Community of the Church (cf. *LG* 9). Pope Francis echoes St Paul in insisting that our very experience of joy "urges us on" (*2 Co* 5:14) to share that joy with others - or it should do so! (*EG* no. 9). If we really believed and lived what we say we believe about the new life that Christ brought us from the Father in the Spirit, then we would surely want others to know about the joy of that life.

With this in mind, let us read a further section from the introduction to Pope Francis's text. **Read nos. 9-10.**

Pause now to reflect and note something from what you have read, a specific phrase or sentence, that strikes you as important and which you would like to highlight.

Pope Francis tells us that "the Gospel offers us the chance to live on a higher plane". Communicating this truth to others, he says, is the source of our own fulfilment. In other words, the more we live our lives so that others may know Christ, the more we ourselves discover the richness of life. The world of today is in great need of heralds of the Good News whose lives "glow with fervour" from the joy of knowing Christ.

We learn from the Scriptures

Pope Francis writes of "an evangelising community" (no. 24). Such a community "goes forth". Since the Lord has loved us first and unconditionally, this community takes the initiative in reaching out to others. For the same reason, it has an endless desire to show mercy. It gets involved in, and is supportive of the lives of others by both word and deed, touching "the flesh of the suffering Christ in others".

It waits patiently, grounded in what he calls "apostolic endurance", not being governed by time. It bears fruit and rejoices; and its joy, says the Pope, "becomes beauty in the liturgy", a beauty which lies at the source of the Church's own self-giving (see no. 24).

Let us listen to what St Luke says of the early Church.

Read: Acts 2:42-47.

Here we see the first Christian Community, gathered around the Apostles, being drawn together not only by teaching and fellowship, but in the "breaking of bread and prayers" of the liturgy; they share their goods with glad and generous hearts; and they reach out to others, who in turn enter into joyful communion with them.

We find another wonderfully evocative picture in the First Letter of St John, in which he ardently affirms: "[We] proclaim to you the eternal life which was with the Father and was made manifest to us...so that you may have fellowship with us; and our fellowship is with the Father and with his Son, Jesus Christ. We are writing this that our joy may be complete" (*1 Jn* 1:2-4).

These passages from Scripture express the deepest mystery of the Church, a mystery of communion made real in and by the Eucharist. Yet, can these descriptions be compatible with what we see around us: members of the Church displaying a lack of faith and of love; sinful clergy and laity; dissidence and disobedience...? Pope Francis does not want us to be "robbed of our joy" by the sad fact of sin in the Church (no. 83). Guided by the teaching of the Second Vatican Council, let us always remember that the Church - thanks to her union with Christ - is mysteriously composed of both human and divine elements:

- As the Body of Christ (sacramentally one with him), the Church is unfailingly holy; she lives only from God.

- At the same time, as the Bride of Christ (called to an ever-closer union with her Bridegroom), the Church is in constant need of purification and renewal.

- Yet, these are not *two* churches: an invisible (holy) Church, and a visible (sinful) institution. There is only one Church, with both human and divine elements (*LG* 7-8).
  "This mystery is a profound one," affirms St Paul strongly, "and I am saying that it refers to Christ and the Church" (*Ep* 5:32).

God's divine light and life came through the humanity of the Son; now they are communicated to us not despite but through the human elements of the Church. The "flesh and blood" of the Church can indeed be a scandal, a stumbling-block, as Christ's humanity was a scandal for those who did not believe in him. Furthermore, whereas Christ did not sin, we his members do. The existence of sin within the Church (Benedict XVI called it "filth") can be a real obstacle for us, unless we see the Church through the eyes of faith and love her as Christ loved her: he died and delivered himself up *for her* (*Ep* 5:27).

Pope Francis wants us to be mindful of what he calls this "mystical, contemplative fraternity" (no. 92), whilst looking honestly at those aspects of the life of the Church (in our own lives first!) which may obstruct the proclamation of the Gospel today (nos. 92-101). "Let us not allow ourselves to be robbed of community!" he pleads.

We learn from St Francis

St Francis was deeply concerned that his disciples should live together in joy. But he knew that they, too, would feel the effects of sin amongst them. Having responded so generously to the Lord's command to "rebuild the Church", Francis soon attracted men from all walks of life who desired to imitate him in prayer, penance and work for the Church. As these followers became more numerous, Francis took his community to Rome to have their way of life officially approved by Pope Innocent III, an approval he received in 1209. Just two years later, he and St Clare co-founded the female branch of the Order, "the Poor Ladies of San Damiano". These communities continue to this day to "rebuild the Church" after the example of St Francis.

From the beginning, Francis recognised the importance of working with others in order to serve the Lord. Accordingly, in the Franciscan tradition, the apostolate is never an isolated process; rather, friars preach and serve in groups, or at least in pairs. St Francis looked upon the members of his community as a gift from God; he would later write very simply in his Testament: "The Lord gave me brethren".

Yet Francis was not naïve; he appreciated that communal life was challenging, and that it is often hardest to treat those *closest* to us with respect. Accordingly, in the Rule he composed for his community, he devoted an entire chapter to the compassion the brothers should show each other. He exhorted them to "love one another, as the Lord says: 'This is my commandment, that you love one another, as I have loved you'. Let them show their love by the works they do for each other."

We reflect

The theme of this present chapter, "The Joy of Life Together in Christ" sums up Chapter Two of the Exhortation. Here, Pope Francis presents the main challenge we face today, which he himself calls the "crisis of communal commitment". This, he says, not only wounds relationships in the world, but it deeply affects relationships within the Church. After an important introduction (nos. 50-51), Chapter Two has two parts.

- In nos. 52-75, Pope Francis depicts aspects of the crisis of commitment which weaken the Church's mission because they "threaten the life and dignity of God's people";

- In nos. 76-109, he discusses things which "affect those who are directly involved in the Church's institutions and in her work of evangelisation", causing them to lose sight of the mystery of communion which they are called to serve and proclaim.

Pause here to review the headings of Chapter Two found in the contents pages, in order to gain an overview of this part of the Exhortation.

There is so much in this chapter. Where do we start? It will help to recall something quoted at the start of this session: "The Church shines forth as 'people made one by the unity of the Father, the Son, and the Spirit'" (St Cyprian, *LG* 4). When we say we are made in the image and likeness of God, we need to remember that this means in the image and likeness *of the Blessed Trinity*, the three Persons in one God. Our unity, our oneness is, then, a call to *communion*, where "the one and the many" coexist in a wonderful harmony of mutual love, as in the life of God.

Only the Blessed Trinity knows the perfect bliss of this communion, in which each person is loved by the others unconditionally, personally and fruitfully. Our daily experience is that that this is far from being the case on earth. Despite undeniable progress today, there exist what the Pope calls "new and often anonymous kinds of power" (no. 52). He strongly shouts "No!" to "certain factors which can restrain or weaken the impulse of missionary renewal in the Church", coming either from within or without. No! to all forms of exclusion; to the idolatry of money; to all systems which rule rather than serve; to inequalities which spawn violence; to selfishness and sloth; to sterile pessimism; to spiritual worldliness; to warring among ourselves (nos. 53-60).

Is there a "Yes!" to counter these aberrations? Indeed. It lies precisely in the new relationships brought about by Christ's redemptive work, uniting us to the Trinity. Pope Francis describes this as true Christian Humanism, "the unified and complete sense of human life that the Gospel proposes" (no. 75). Our world needs this more than anything else; it is, in fact, the only thing the Church has to offer (cf. also no. 264). It is imperative *for the sake of the world* that the Church, the Kingdom of God in its beginnings on earth (cf. *LG* 7), should allow the Blessed Trinity to live their communion in her and through her. We say "allow", since God will not force our free will. It is for us to trust the Lord, "allowing" him to lead us into ever deeper communion. Only then will the human race, in all its diversity, experience the wonderful union - *communion* - for which it was created. Our fidelity to the will of God has truly cosmic implications (cf. no. 216).

In what Pope Francis calls the "spiritual desertification" (no. 86) of today's world, our mission is to be "living sources of water from which others can drink", pointing to the only true hope which can never be stifled. The

Church offers humanity "true faith in the incarnate Son of God"; a faith which is "inseparable from self-giving, from membership in the community, from service, from reconciliation with others" (no. 88), precisely because the Church's proclamation of the faith wells up from her life of communion in the Blessed Trinity. Pope Francis condenses his thoughts in a remarkable phrase: "The Son of God, by becoming flesh, summoned us to the revolution of tenderness" (no. 88).

Questions for reflection

1. "If we wish to lead a dignified and fulfilling life, we have to reach out to others and seek their good" (no. 9). How can your life with others be such as to strengthen your witness to the Good News of life together in Christ? Think of concrete places and situations, such as in the family, at work, in the shops, on the bus or train, and so forth.

2. "Life grows by being given away, it weakens in isolation and comfort" (no. 10). When have you experienced the truth of this yourself? What lessons can you draw from this?

3. "Not to share one's wealth with the poor is to steal from them and to take away their livelihood. It is not our own goods which we hold, but theirs" (no. 57). Are there any implications for yourself or your family here?

4. Thinking again of Acts 2:42-47, reflect on your parish in the areas of teaching, liturgy, prayer, life together, and mission; consider *one area* where your common parish life in Christ could be further enriched.

Meditation and final prayer

As we conclude, we turn to the Lord. First, let us read prayerfully *CCC* 771.

Pause for silent reflection

We pray the *Our Father*

O God, who have taught your Church
to keep all the heavenly commandments
by loving you and loving our neighbour,
grant us a spirit of peace and grace,
so that your entire family
may be devoted to you wholeheartedly
and united in purity of intent.
Through our Lord Jesus Christ, your Son.

(Collect for Promoting Harmony)

Chapter 5: The Joy of the Herald

*"My mouth will tell of your righteous acts,
of your deeds of salvation all the day"* (Ps 70:15).

The theme of this chapter is the joy of being a
herald, someone who proclaims the Good News of
Jesus Christ. Chapter Three of *Evangelii Gaudium*
is dedicated to "The Proclamation of the Gospel".
The psalmist says, "My mouth will tell of your
righteous acts". So we ask: Of what do I tell with
my mouth? How much do I use it for proclaiming
God's "righteous acts"? Am I confident in being
able to speak of these "righteous acts" and "deeds
of salvation"?

We pray *The Benedictus*

We read the text

As we continue our exploration of *Evangelii Gaudium*,
let us read nos. 11-13 where the focus is on the message
we proclaim. Pope Francis begins by speaking of the
importance of a renewal of preaching; he then looks at the
central message the Church proclaims.

Pause now to reflect and note something from what you have read, a specific phrase or sentence, that strikes you as important and which you would like to highlight.

The heading for these paragraphs is "Eternal newness", an expression Pope Francis is using to sum up the essence of the Good News we proclaim. You may have noticed that Pope Francis takes us to scriptural passages from Revelation and Hebrews in which we read that Christ is the "eternal Gospel", "the same yesterday, today and forever" (no. 11). "Gospel" comes from the old English for *god spel*, meaning 'good story or message'. Christ himself *is* the good message, the Good News, the Gospel we proclaim. "Eternal newness" refers to that which is beyond time and never changes. How, then, can Christ be the *Eternal* Good News? Only if he is God. This, indeed, is the truth. Christ is the eternal Son of God, beyond time, and beyond change: "God from God, Light from Light, true God from true God", as Christians have professed each Sunday in the Creed for two thousand years.

Why is this section called eternal *newness*?

Let us pause and take note of all the instances where the terms 'new', 'renew' and 'newness' are used in these paragraphs.

'New' is a prominent word in Scripture. Indeed, it is the word we use to refer to the inspired writings of Christ's disciples, the "New" Testament. These documents refer to the central act which we celebrate every Sunday at Mass, that of Christ bringing about a "*new* covenant" in his blood (cf. *Lk* 22:20; *1 Co* 11:25). The New Testament also speaks frequently of the *new life* Christ came to bring us (cf. *Ga* 6:15; *2 Co* 5:17; *Ep* 2:15).

In the Greek New Testament, there are two different words for 'new': *Neos* meaning young; new, as compared to old; it carries with it connotations of vigour and freshness. Pope Francis refers to this kind of newness when he says that the Christian message "will never grow old" (no. 11). But this is not the principal kind of newness, for in these same paragraphs he insists that memory, history and Tradition are all crucial to the Church. He reminds us that the "new covenant" is in fact an act of remembrance, and he describes the believer as "one who remembers" (no. 13). Finally, he speaks of the importance of returning to "the source…to recover the Gospel's original freshness" (no. 11).

The other Greek word used in the New Testament to mean "new" is *kainos*. This refers to the newness of something that is of another order, a different nature; it is the newness of something wholly other, a divine presence. St John speaks of this when he says that since Jesus came "from above", that is "from God", he "utters the words of God" (*Jn* 3:31,34). The newness Christ brings is the very presence of the Lord God among us. It is to this newness that Pope Francis is drawing our attention - the amazing fact of the newness of God's own presence with us, in the person of Jesus Christ. The Good News is that God has "visited his people and redeemed them", as we pray in the *Benedictus*. The Lord has not just sent a messenger: he himself has appeared in our midst to save us!

We learn from the Scriptures

In the Gospel accounts, the one who gives the message of the Good News is called a 'herald'. In the Greek New Testament, the word for this messenger or herald, is *keryx*, and the fundamental Gospel message the herald announces is called the *kerygma*. The kerygma is the expression of the essence, the very *heart* of the Christian faith. This kerygma, Pope Francis reminds us all, "needs to be at the centre of all evangelising activity and all efforts at Church renewal" (no. 164).

There are three elements which are always communicated when expressing the kerygma:

- The life and love of the Blessed Trinity;

- The saving work of Jesus Christ, Second Person of the Trinity;

- The new life made available and bestowed on us.

We find this kerygma expressed in a number of different ways by the Church: in her Scriptures, her Creeds, and her Catechisms. See, for example, the following:

- "God so loved the world that he gave his only Son, so that whoever believes in him may not perish, but have eternal life" (*Jn* 3:16);

- "In Christ, God was reconciling the world to himself, not counting their trespass against them, and entrusting to us the message of reconciliation" (*2 Co* 5:19);

- "When the fullness of time had come, God sent his Son as Redeemer and Saviour. In his Son and through him, he invites us to become, in the Holy Spirit, his adopted children and thus heirs of his blessed life" (*CCC* 1).

In the *Benedictus*, we can see that Zechariah is a herald of God's deeds of salvation: "Blessed be the Lord the God of Israel, he has visited his people and redeemed them".

The angel Gabriel who announced the birth of Jesus to Mary comes to her as a herald of the Gospel, his first word being "Rejoice!" In Greek, the word rejoice is related to the word for grace. Mary can rejoice because God has filled her with his grace and will himself take flesh in her womb. She will be what the Church calls "the God-bearer" - *Theotokos*, in Greek. Mary's rejoicing is unique, since only she literally 'bore God himself' in the flesh. Yet, every Christian is also called, like Mary, to rejoice because of the new life of grace God has given to each one of us.

Each Christian is also called to be a herald of the amazing news that the eternal Son of God came among us to save us and make us the Father's adopted children in the Holy Spirit. The call to become heralds of the Gospel was given to all of us by Christ after his resurrection. "Our mandate," says Pope Francis, "is to 'go into all the world and proclaim the good news to the whole creation' (*Mk* 16:15)" (no. 181).

Read: Matthew 28:18-20

Pope Francis draws our attention to this passage on a number of occasions (cf. nos. 113, 120, 160, 162). What are some of the points that he particularly wishes us to appreciate?

- The message is given with the full authority of God, which Christ says has been given to him. The announcement is a divine message of happiness, a gift from above. Pope Francis warns us: "We receive the message of the Gospel as a gift and we should transmit it as a gift, but not as something of our own: it is a received gift that we give." In transmitting it, we are then "to be faithful. Because we have received and we should give a Gospel that is not ours, it is of Jesus".

- In the work of evangelisation, God acts first, he takes the initiative. He has indeed "loved us first" (*1 Jn* 4:19; no. 12). "God, by his sheer grace, draws us to himself and makes us one with him" (no. 160). Following the Tradition of the Church, Pope Francis describes this as "the priority of grace" (nos. 12, 112, 162). This is underlined very clearly in Jesus's command to baptise, for baptism is God's free gift.

- Jesus's command is to "make disciples". Making disciples means teaching people to know, love and follow the Lord in his Church evermore closely. As Pope Francis says, evangelisation calls for a "process of ongoing formation and maturation" (no. 160). This leads to a life in "the Spirit", attentive to God's grace for a "constant sanctification which pleases God and gives him glory" (no. 162).

- Jesus's call is universal, it is for "all nations". God who created all, invites everyone to respond to his work of salvation. He calls us not merely as individuals, but as a people: "This people which God has chosen and called is the Church" (no. 113).

We learn from St Francis

A little after his conversion, as Francis was walking through a wood, thieves fell upon him and demanded to know who he was. He answered boldly and prophetically: "I am the herald of the great King". Heralds announce news, they always speak in the name of another.

Having abandoned his worldly ambitions in order to imitate Christ more perfectly, Francis began a life of fervent prayer and selfless work for the poor. Yet, as time progressed, he realised that he was called to galvanise others to holiness not just by the striking witness of his holy life but also by words. One of Francis's miracles, recorded in the biography written by St Bonaventure, is the silencing of the swallows: Francis commanded them to stop interrupting his sermon, and they immediately obeyed him! This episode is often seen as illustrating the unique relationship Francis had with creation; more importantly, it shows that much of the saint's time and energy was spent in touring Italy preaching and teaching the Good News.

Francis loved preaching. It is a popular misunderstanding that Francis said, 'Preach the Gospel and, if you have to, use words!' In fact, Francis knew that words accompanied deeds, explaining them and leading others to appreciate their true meaning; for him, as a disciple of the Lord - the Word who became flesh - words and deeds belong together.

We reflect

The three paragraphs from *Evangelii Gaudium* that we read today are very encouraging for us and provide important insights:

- When we really "hear" and experience the truths of God, they are always new.

- We cannot be heralds unless we first receive from God what he wants us to receive and know for ourselves. When we ourselves have had the joy of understanding and appreciating the "righteous acts" of the Father in the work of the Holy Spirit and his "deeds of salvation" in Christ, then we want to pass this message on to others.

- We receive from God by drawing from sources such as the Bible; the sacraments, especially Holy Mass; and the *Catechism of the Catholic Church*. We are then to keep what God gives in the memory of our hearts, as Mary did (*Lk* 2:19, 51), in order to be able remind ourselves regularly of God's words and deeds (no. 142).

To be heralds in the everyday circumstances of life the *first step*, then, is to receive for oneself.

The *second step* is, for example, to practise each day saying something good about what God has done. That might be: "Thank God, the weather is good today"; "Thank God, the bus was on time for my aunt to get to the doctor"; "God sent his angels to protect me from a crazy driver!"; "By God's grace, I didn't get angry and stayed calm"; "God is always merciful, and he gives us the strength to be merciful too".

We are heralds when we speak like this. It is a happy way of looking at life, for it is the most deeply true way of seeing things. When we are tempted to moan or complain, let's ask the Holy Spirit to turn us towards the beautiful things he is doing, rather than to what we are not doing, or not doing well.

The *third step* is to practise announcing the kerygma. We do so when, as simply and as naturally as possible, we say what we believe to our children, our family and our friends.

Questions for reflection

1. What point from this session has helped you to appreciate even more the joy of being heralds of Christ, the great King?

2. To whom are we to be heralds? How might we carry out this task? Consider the following: "In what might be regarded as the domestic Church, parents, by word and example, are the first heralds of the faith with regard to their children".[8] "May the Lord make all of you enthusiastic heralds of the Gospel in the new '*agora*' which the current media are opening up".[9]

3. In your own life, what are some of the "righteous acts" of the Lord, some of the good things he has done and which you would like to share?

4. Practise expressing the kerygma in a way that is natural to you.

Meditation and final prayer

As we conclude, we turn to the Lord. First, let us read prayerfully *CCC* 425.

Pause for silent reflection

We pray the *Our Father*

Enable us, we pray, almighty God,
to proclaim the power of the risen Lord,
that we, who have received the pledge of his gift,
may come to possess all he gives when it is
fully revealed.
Through our Lord Jesus Christ, your son,
who lives and reigns with you in the unity of
the Holy Spirit,
one God, for ever and ever. Amen.

(Collect for Tuesday after Second Sunday of Easter)

Chapter 6: The Joy of those who Love the Poor Christ

"Come, O blessed of my Father, inherit the kingdom prepared for you from the foundation of the world... Truly, I say to you, as you did it to one of the least of these my brethren, you did it for me"
(*Mt* 25:34,40).

St Paul reminds us that "God has no favourites" (*Rm* 2:11). That is because each one of us is God's favourite! We are all equally precious in the eyes of our Creator, whatever our race, age, state of health, way of life, social status, or creed. God desires only one thing: to prepare each one of us - from the youngest foetus, to the oldest man or woman in the world - to be gathered into his loving and eternal embrace. When we judge either our own worth or that of someone else according to anything other than God's measureless love, we judge falsely. Yet, we so often fall into evaluating ourselves and others according to social position, achievements, connections, wealth, or health. Pope Francis calls on us to know the unique joy of loving others and ourselves *as God loves us*, and to make that joy real, through the way we treat others and even ourselves. We are utterly precious in the eyes of the Lord.

We pray *The Benedictus*

We read the text

Let us continue our exploration of *Evangelii Gaudium*, by reading nos. 14-15. These paragraphs do not at first seem to be related to the love of the poor, and yet they are. They speak of the different states of spiritual neediness of all people, be they materially rich or poor. The paragraphs speak of a "summons" to love people in "three principal settings".

Pause now to reflect and note something from what you have read, a specific phrase or sentence, that strikes you as important and which you would like to highlight.

The Good News of God's redeeming love in Jesus Christ is like a "delicious banquet", says Pope Francis; it is food for the starving, made most fully present in the Eucharist. The image of a feast is one Jesus himself often used in his teaching (see *Mt* 22:1-14; *Lk* 14:7-14). But the invitation to eat freely of the food at this banquet is only accepted by those who want it because they know their need of God and of the food only he can give; they recognise that without the solid food of his love, they will always be poor.

Jesus showed us this truth through the circumstances of his birth. As he was born in poverty in a manger in Bethlehem, so is he 'born' today only in hearts and minds which are 'mangers' - that is, open to receive a kind of food they know they cannot produce for themselves; as 'mangers', they know they are only wood and straw.

God came to earth unexpectedly as a child, in poverty. The shepherds and wise men saw the truth: they came to adore, kneeling before him in his poverty. You may have noticed that, whenever an altar is prepared for Mass, a simple white cloth is laid on the altar stone. Christian art depicting the Nativity often shows the Infant Jesus lying on just such a cloth. This is to remind us that we, today - modern shepherds and sages - come to Mass to adore and worship Jesus, the Incarnate Son, hidden in the poverty of the word and of the small white Host. With these, he gives the food which satisfies our hunger for his love, that which "comes down from heaven" (*Jn* 6:33,38,41,42,50,51,58).

The first group of people to whom Pope Francis refers in no. 15 are those who need to have their hearts constantly lit up with this truth. These need the work of on-going evangelisation that is the "ordinary pastoral ministry" of the local church.

Pope Francis refers to a second situation, a second group of people, who also experience a second area of spiritual poverty, but of a different kind (no. 15). This is precisely the group who are in need of a 'new evangelisation'. He is referring to the baptised who "lack a meaningful relationship to the Church". They are most especially to be loved, since they no longer experience what Pope Francis calls "the consolation of the faith". Jesus is present in his Body on the altar; he is also present in his Body, the Church. He even remains present in this group of the baptised "whose lives do not reflect the demands of Baptism" since they do not participate actively in the life of the Church. Pope Francis says very strongly: "It is an absurd dichotomy to love Christ without the Church; to listen to Christ, but not to the Church; to be with Christ at the edge of the Church. It can't be done". When Jesus appeared to Saul, for example, who was persecuting the early Christians, he challenged him: "Saul, Saul," he said, "Why are you persecuting me?" Saul's passionate hatred of Christians turned into an ardent love for the Church after this meeting with the Risen Lord. From then on, Paul loved Jesus in his Body, the Church, convinced as he had become that Jesus himself "loved the Church and delivered himself up for her" (*Ep* 5:25-27). This is why Pope Francis insists that the Church, in her "maternal concern, tries to help them experience a conversion which will restore the joy of faith to their hearts and inspire a commitment to the Gospel" (no. 15).

There is yet a third category of people: "Those who do not know Jesus Christ or who have always rejected him" (no. 15). People can be poor in many different ways - poor in the material goods of this world, poor in health, poor in friends, poor in expectations for the future, and so forth. Yet, Blessed Mother Teresa, coming from the slums of Calcutta, once said that she had never encountered such poverty as that she found in the materially rich countries of the West. Here, she found there the deepest forms of poverty among people who, though rich in the world's eyes, were poor in hope, poor in faith, poor in love.

Pope Francis insists that every one of these people, so desperately poor, has the "right to receive the Gospel". Every person, whatever their life circumstances, can receive these true riches, "the greatest of which is love" (*1 Co* 13:13). Christians have the duty to proclaim the joy of the Gospel "without excluding anyone". Nothing, says St Paul, can separate us from the love of God communicated in Christ (*Rm* 8:35-39). This love overcomes all - the greatest joy in heaven being provoked by the "sinner who repents"!

We learn from the Scriptures

The preciousness of every person in the eyes of God is one of Scripture's fundamental teachings. All human beings are made in the image and likeness of God, all are called to eternal life in Christ. And since God's love is without reservation or exception, so should our love be: "Beloved, if God so loved us, we also ought to love one another" (*1 Jn* 4:11).

Jesus spoke of the two great commandments, summing up all of the demands in the first Testament, as those of love of God and love of neighbour (*Mk* 12:28-34). The Apostles taught that one cannot claim to know the love of God unless one shows this in the love of neighbour. St John even goes as far as to write: "If anyone says, 'I love God,' and hates his brother, he is a liar; for he who does not love his brother whom he has seen, cannot love God whom he has not seen" (*1 Jn* 4:20).

The love of one's neighbour is described in the Scriptures as "the royal law" (*Jm* 2:8). It is the law of the Kingdom of God, the law befitting those called to be adopted sons and daughters of the divine King. We show that we are following this law when we treat every single person with the dignity that is theirs as such a son or daughter.

Read: James 2:1-9

We learn from St Francis

St Francis's love for the poor is well known. Like Blessed Mother Teresa of Calcutta, his zeal in serving his afflicted neighbour sprang from his conviction that he encountered Christ himself in society's rejects: the sick, the imprisoned, the materially poor. On this, Christ had been unequivocal: "As you did it to one of the least of these my brethren," he said, "you did it for me" (*Mt* 25:40). St Francis's attitude is illustrated in the way he reprimanded one of the friars who had harshly repulsed a beggar. When Francis heard of this, he commanded the brother to prostrate himself at the feet of the beggar, humbly acknowledging his fault, and seeking the beggar's pardon and prayers. When the friar had done this, Francis told him, "Whenever you see a poor man, consider the poverty of Our Lord and of his Mother. Similarly, when you see a sick person, remember the infirmities that Christ took upon himself".

St Francis considered it crucial for any follower of Jesus to be concerned with both the material and the spiritual needs of others. He was always seeking to supply the needs of the poor, and maintained that not to provide for the needy when one could do so was equivalent to theft.

We reflect

Pope Francis reminds us forcefully that alongside our proclamation of the Good News of God's redeeming love, we are to seek ways of making the truth of God's Kingdom a reality both in our personal relationships and in the structures of society (nos. 182-184). This is in keeping with the vision and values we find throughout Scripture, in the life of St Francis and the other saints, and in the great Social Teaching of the Church. In the Exhortation itself, it is the topic of Chapter Four, "The Social Dimension of Evangelisation".

The chapter takes up the theme of loving the "poor Christ", whether that poverty be material or spiritual. For there to develop a genuine love for the word's poor, what is called for, says Pope Francis, is a new vision of humanity. We are to learn to see through God's eyes, and to do so by having the mind "which was in Jesus Christ" (*Ph* 2:5). Only thus will we recognise things in their rightful perspective, which is to say, God's. The love we have for each person will then be true, for we shall perceive that "he or she is beautiful above and beyond mere appearances" (no. 199).

There are practical implications which follow from this renewed vision of each person, and Pope Francis identifies some of these in this chapter. We will:

• Place greater value on people rather than on things;

• Give more value to relationships than to maintaining our distance from people and protecting our free time;

• Pay more practical attention to those in different kinds of poverty, to befriend them, take up their cause, and listen sincerely to them;

• Support welfare projects and ways of ridding society of unjust inequalities;

• Provide a voice for the most vulnerable and defenceless, all those who experience rejection or exclusion, such as the pre-born, the elderly, and all anonymous victims of human trafficking;

• Take time to find real, long-term solutions to the problems of society, not merely temporary measures aimed at quick political gains.

Questions for reflection

1. Go through the list above, and see which are most present as kinds of poverty in your local community. As Christ's Body, to which of these can you respond, and what are some concrete responses you can make?

2. Evangelisers are those who wish to share their joy by inviting others "to a delicious banquet". Do you need to grow in your own love of the Eucharist and the other sacraments in order to be able to experience these as 'delicious banquets'? Is this how you see the sacraments - Baptism, Holy Mass, Confession, Confirmation, and so on? Do you describe them as such to others?

3. Evangelisers are people who wish to share their joy by pointing to "an horizon of beauty". Is there anything in the life of the Church that you enjoy as beautiful, and to which you would like to invite other people? Is your Church beautiful, for example? Is there something in it which gives you joy, and which you could point out to someone else - e.g. a particular statue, or stained glass window? Is there a joyful group in your parish into which you could invite someone who is lapsed? Is there beautiful Christian music? Are there beautiful times of prayer?

4. What have I heard from this session that has been important to me, helping me to see how to grow in the joy of loving the "poor Christ"?

Meditation and final prayer

As we conclude, we turn to the Lord. First, let us read prayerfully *CCC* 2443-2444.

Pause for silent reflection

We pray the *Our Father*

O God, who have taught your Church
to keep all the heavenly commandments
by love of you as God and love of neighbour;
Grant that, practising the works of charity
we may be worthy to be numbered
among the blessed in your Kingdom.
Through our Lord Jesus Christ, your Son,
who lives and reigns with you in the unity of
the Holy Spirit,
one God, for ever and ever. Amen.

(Collect for those who practise works of mercy)

Chapter 7: The Joy of Mary, Star of the New Evangelisation

"Rejoice greatly, O daughter of Zion!
Shout aloud, O daughter of Jerusalem!
Behold, your king comes to you" (Zc 9:9).

In these chapters, we have been trying to grasp more deeply the joy of the Gospel. In this, the last, we look to Mary who, as the true daughter of Zion, embodies the Scripture passage above. Having received the Good News from the angel, she indeed "rejoiced greatly", proclaiming this joy aloud in the prayer we know as the *Magnificat*. We now read from the final chapter of *Evangelli Gaudium*. Pope Francis concludes with a beautiful prayer of his own, in which he contemplates Mary's unique role in the new evangelisation. He addresses Mary as the "Mother of the living Gospel", meaning of Jesus Christ, which she became by the will of the Father through the action of the Holy Spirit.

We pray *The Magnificat*

We read the text

In *Evangelii Gaudium* no. 18, Pope Francis speaks of a "definite style of evangelisation" which he earnestly asks us to adopt "in every activity". In the final paragraphs of the Exhortation he identifies this style as Mary's way. With Pope Francis, therefore, we can contemplate Mary and her way of rejoicing, her way of recognising "the traces of God's Spirit in events great and small" (no. 288). We read no. 18, and then nos. 287-288.

Pause now to reflect and note something from what you have read, a specific phrase or sentence, that strikes you as important and which you would like to highlight.

We have already touched upon many practical aspects of the "definite style" of evangelisation evoked here by Pope Francis. Now in Chapter Five (nos. 259-288), the Pope takes us to its deep spiritual roots. The chapter is called "Spirit-filled Evangelisers", whose four characteristics he underlines:

- They are people who remain close to the saving presence of Jesus. Rooted in him, they never stray far from his loving and redeeming presence (nos. 264-267);

- United with Jesus, they are able to remain close to his people, allowing Jesus to reach through them each person with his love (nos. 268-274);

- They have confidence in the hidden but real work of redemption which Jesus continues to carry out in the world, learning to interpret events in the light of his paschal mystery, his Passion, death and resurrection (nos. 275-280);

- They pray constantly for others, learning to be thankful for the gift of each, all the while asking the Blessed Trinity to bless and redeem each person, each relationship and every situation (nos. 281-283).

In the final section of both Chapter Five and of the Exhortation itself, Pope Francis takes us to Mary, without whom, he says, "we could never truly understand the spirit of the new evangelisation" (no. 284). He shows us how each of the above four characteristics is exemplified in Mary's life in a perfect way. She is the one who, before and for all others, remains close to Jesus and leads us into his presence. She is not only his mother, but was given to be our mother too, and remains personally close to each one of us. She had the courage to stand by her Son's cross and share in his Passion in a unique way, as his mother. Finally, she is the great intercessor whom Pope Francis invokes for the work of the new evangelisation (no. 287).

Her unique grace is to be, physically, the mother of Someone who is God. This great mystery took place with her freely willed co-operation, but it was accomplished by the action of God alone. Thanks to Mary's Yes, the Son of

God now shares our human nature. This is the heart of our faith, the kernel of what it is we are to proclaim in the new Evangelisation. John of the Cross puts it as only a poet (and a saint!) can:

> For with her co-operation
> This great mystery could be.
> With her flesh the Word was clothed
> By the Blessed Trinity…Hers His flesh
> and hers His dwelling
> 'Ere His human life began,
> Wherefore He is called together
> Son of God and Son of Man.[10]

We learn from the Scriptures

Mary shows us the way to rejoice. She also shows us the way, the 'style' or spirituality, of the new evangelisation. She, more than anyone else, is the "Spirit-filled evangeliser". Every member of the Church is called to be "Marian", and Pope Francis leads us to some key passages from the Scriptures to explain how this is the case.

Read: Acts 1:12-14; 2:1-4

At the beginning of Chapter Five, Pope Francis invites us to consider this great event of Pentecost. In its light, he writes:

- "Spirit-filled evangelisers means evangelisers fearlessly open to the working of the Holy Spirit" (no. 259);

- "A Spirit-filled evangelisation is one guided by the Holy Spirit" (no. 261);

- Our lives must be "transfigured by God's presence" through the action of the Spirit "for he is the soul of the Church called to proclaim the Gospel" (nos. 259, 261).

It is our response to the action of the Holy Spirit which mysteriously allows God to bring about a people, rich in diversity, yet "made one with the unity of the Father, the Son and the Spirit" (St Cyprian; cf. *LG* 4). And it is membership of this people which gives "shape" to both our evangelising (nos. 268, 270-274) and to our prayer of intercession (nos. 281-282).

As a member of this people - the Church - we are invited to love the Son and everything he loves (nos. 264, 265): first and foremost, his Father and the glory that belongs uniquely to him (no. 267; *Jn* 17:24). In the same "seamless-garment" movement, we are to love the world and everything it contains, particularly human beings at every stage of their existence (nos. 268, 274). This is radically impossible, unless we actively seek to live under the action of the Holy Spirit, to live not only *for* God in generosity, but *from* God in humble obedience to him.

It is the Spirit who, by revealing Jesus, the Son (*Jn* 14:16,26), brings us to the fullest knowledge and love of the Father; it is the Spirit who gives a taste for the "newness" of the Gospel and its beauty (nos. 259, 264);

it is the Spirit who makes us instruments in *his* reaching out to "his people", especially to the most dispossessed or rejected, those experiencing poverty under all its forms (no. 268, cf. *Ex* 3:6-10).

We must be convinced that there is something absolutely unique about Jesus Christ. Without this conviction and love, we will convince no one - perhaps not even ourselves (no. 266). At work in us is the power of Christ's resurrection, "a vital power which has permeated this world…as an irresistible force" *today* (no. 276). This enables us to overcome difficulties, for in truth it is not about us: it is about God and the power of his love for all without exception (nos. 263, 277-279).

Let us believe in God. Let us believe in God's Kingdom, present and growing in this world thanks to Christ's resurrection: "Jesus did not rise in vain. This is the source of our hope!" (no. 278).

It is so simple, which is not to say that it is easy. Pope Francis puts it this way: "The Holy Spirit works as he wills, when he wills and where he wills; we entrust ourselves without pretending to see striking results. We know only that our commitment is necessary… There is no greater freedom than that of allowing oneself to be guided by the Holy Spirit… [He] knows well what is needed in every time and place" (nos. 279, 280). Come, Holy Spirit!

We learn from St Francis

St Francis was a man of great prayer, intuitively responsive to the movements of the Holy Spirit in his life. A lesser-known aspect of his spiritual life is his deep love for the Blessed Virgin. He placed himself trustingly under the powerful intercession of Mary, the spiritual mother of every Christian. St Bonaventure, in his famous biography of St Francis, records that "he [Francis] bore unspeakable love for the Mother of our Lord, Jesus Christ, because by her the Lord of Majesty became our Brother, and through her we have obtained mercy. In her, next to Christ, he placed his confidence; he took her for his advocate, and in her honour he was accustomed to fast devoutly." Francis composed various prayers to her, one of which he called his *Salutation to the Blessed Virgin Mary*:

> Hail, holy Lady! Most holy Queen,
> Mother of God, Mary!
> Though art ever-Virgin, elected by the most
> holy Father of Heaven,
> consecrated by His most Holy and Beloved Son,
> and by the Holy Spirit, the Paraclete;
> in thee is and was the plentitude of all grace
> and good!...
> Most holy Mother of our Lord, Jesus Christ,
> spouse of the Holy Spirit,
> pray for us to thy beloved Son, our Lord and Master,

together with St Michael the Archangel,
and all the Angels and Saints of Heaven. Amen.

We reflect

Pope Francis is following in the footsteps of St Francis and of so many great saints in according this central place to Mary. It is no coincidence that both the Exhortation and the document from the Second Vatican Council, *Lumen Gentium*, which is the background to it (no. 17), concludes by turning to Our Blessed Lady.

When, in its final two chapters, *Lumen Gentium* asks where the Church is to be found - that People of God whom it has contemplated so deeply - it gives two answers: it is found to be a "pilgrim People", journeying towards the Blessed Trinity, with members on earth, others undergoing the purification of love in purgatory, and still others already taken up in the vision of her Lord. But there is one person whom the Church sees going ahead of herself in every age and who never abandons her. Someone in whom the Church fully recognises herself: a woman who is a unique member of this People; who is Virgin and Mother, before and for the Church; "spotless and without blemish" (*Ep* 5:27), for and before the Church; a faithful disciple who believes, who hopes, who loves and serves; and who is already assumed body and soul into heaven, from where she intercedes for this People with all the tenderness of a mother's affection, seeing us only in her Son.

This is Mary, the Mother of God (cf. *Lk* 1:43). At the end of the Council, Pope Paul VI, whom as we have seen Pope Francis quotes repeatedly throughout his Exhortation, gave her a new title: "Mother of the Church": Mother, he said, of the whole People of God, Mother of the members of her Son's Body, and of all those called to be his members. Jesus himself revealed this on the cross: "Behold, your mother" (*Jn* 19:27), he said to the beloved disciple. Immediately after saying this, he solemnly declared that "everything is now accomplished" (v. 30).

In speaking of Mary's relationship with the Church, Hans Urs von Balthasar goes so far as to say that between Mary and the Church there really is only one mystery: that of the virgin mother who gives birth to the Son of God.

In a fascinating piece, G.K. Chesterton reflects on his own journey into the Church of Rome, and recalls what a pivotal role Mary played in this.[11] Referring to "things Catholic", he writes:

"Now I can scarcely remember a time when the image of Our Lady did not stand up in my mind quite definitely, at the mention or the thought of all these things... I never doubted that this figure (Mary) was the figure of the Faith; that she embodied, as a complete human being still only human, all that this Thing had to say to humanity.

"The instant I remembered the Catholic Church, I remembered her; when I tried to forget the Catholic Church, I tried to forget her; when I finally saw what was nobler than my fate, the freest and the hardest of all my acts of freedom, it was in front of a gilded and very gaudy little image of her in the port of Brindisi, that I promised the thing that I would do, if I returned to my own land."

Mary truly is, in Pope Francis's words, the Star of the New Evangelisation, going ahead of the Pilgrim People of God towards the Father's infinite mercy:

- For who, more than she, lived under the action of the Holy Spirit (*Lk* 1:35);

- Who, more than she, knew Jesus, and through him the Father (*Lk* 2:19);

- Who, more than she, knows that we "have no wine" of joy without her Son (*Jn* 2:3);

- Who, more than she, believed in the resurrection, when even the Apostles themselves doubted (*Jn* 21:6-8);

- And who, better than she, can tell us from the fruit of her own experience that the answer to all our searching and questioning lies in doing "whatever he tells you" (*Jn* 2:5), precisely because "with God, nothing will be impossible" (*Lk* 1:37).

Questions for reflection

1. "There is a Marian 'style' to the Church's work of evangelisation" (no. 288). Which of the aspects of Mary's 'style' to which Pope Francis has drawn our attention would you most like to learn?

2. "Without prolonged moments of adoration, of prayerful encounter with the word, of sincere conversation with the Lord, our work easily becomes meaningless; we lose energy as a result of weariness and difficulties, and our fervor dies out" (no. 262). How can we, individually and as a community, cultivate the moments of prayer and conversation that provide energy for our work of evangelisation?

3. "The missionary's enthusiasm in proclaiming Christ comes from the conviction that he is responding to the deepest yearnings of people's hearts" (cf. no. 265). Think of an example of a yearning in your own life or in the life of someone you know. In what ways does the proclamation of Christ respond to this?

Meditation and final prayer

As we conclude, we turn to the Lord. First, let us read prayerfully CCC 967-968.

Pause for silent reflection

We pray the *Our Father*

Let us conclude our reflections on *The Joy of the Gospel* by turning, as Pope Francis does, to "Mary, Star of the New Evangelisation" in uniting with the whole Church his prayer to "Mary, Virgin and Mother".

Mary, Virgin and Mother,
you who, moved by the Holy Spirit,
welcomed the word of life
in the depths of your humble faith:
as you gave yourself completely to the Eternal One,
help us to say our own "yes"
to the urgent call, as pressing as ever,
to proclaim the good news of Jesus.

Filled with Christ's presence,
you brought joy to John the Baptist,
making him exult in the womb of his mother.
Brimming over with joy,
you sang of the great things done by God.
Standing at the foot of the cross
with unyielding faith,
you received the joyful comfort of the resurrection,
and joined the disciples in awaiting the Spirit
so that the evangelising Church might be born.

Obtain for us now a new ardour born of the
resurrection,
that we may bring to all the Gospel of life
which triumphs over death.
Give us a holy courage to seek new paths,
that the gift of unfading beauty
may reach every man and woman.

Virgin of listening and contemplation,
Mother of love, Bride of the eternal wedding feast,
pray for the Church, whose pure icon you are,
that she may never be closed in on herself
or lose her passion for establishing God's kingdom.

Star of the new evangelisation,
help us to bear radiant witness to communion,
service, ardent and generous faith,
justice and love of the poor,
that the joy of the Gospel
may reach to the ends of the earth,
illuminating even the fringes of our world.

Mother of the living Gospel,
wellspring of happiness for God's little ones,
pray for us.

Amen. Alleluia!

The Fulfilment

Queen of Heaven, Rejoice. Alleluia!

In the same prayer to Our Lady with which we began our reflections on *The Gospel of Joy*, Pope Francis addresses her in these words:

Star of the new evangelisation,
help us to bear radiant witness to communion,
service, ardent and generous faith,
justice and love of the poor,
that the joy of the Gospel
may reach to the ends of the earth,
illuminating even the fringes of our world.

This is what, it seems to us, is depicted in Quarton's striking picture of *The Assumption and Crowning of Our Lady*.[12] Pope Francis has reminded us of the importance of beauty as a means of new evangelisation (no. 167). He was perhaps thinking of such paintings as this.

Before looking at it more deeply, let us recall a biblical scene in which a newly crowned King Solomon is seated on his throne; all his courtiers come in and bow low to pay him homage. Suddenly, his mother, Bathsheba, enters. She has a request on behalf of her other son. Here's what happens: "The king rose to meet her, and bowed down to her; then he sat on his throne, and had a seat brought for the king's mother; and she sat on his right." If this is not remarkable enough, the text continues: "Then she said, 'I have one small request to make of you; do not refuse me.' And the king said to her, 'Make your request, my mother; for I will not refuse you'" (*1 K* 2:19-20).

How tender this is. And if a mere man can be inspired to honour his mother to such a degree, how much more would it not please God the Son to honour his? On ascending to heaven, would he not wait to welcome her, as she had awaited and welcomed him on earth? Would he not share his glory with her, as she had shared her humanity with him? Would he say "no" to her, who had so willingly said "yes" to him? Would he not answer the requests she makes to him, on behalf of all those whom he himself, from the cross, had confided to her to be her children? And would he not present her to humanity as the first fruit of the wonders his grace can do in us, if we would but let him transform us? (cf. *CCC* 721)

In the Preface for the Glory of the Saints, we pray: "In crowning their merits, you crown your own gifts" (St Augustine). Of no one is this more true than of Mary, the person who belongs most to Christ (cf. *1 Co* 15:23) and who, after him, is the highest honour of our race (cf. *Jdt* 15:9).

In his painting, Quarton is professing the Church's faith and his own conviction, that Mary is God's *chef d'œuvre*, his masterpiece (*CCC* 721). The beloved daughter of the Father, the Mother of the Son, the Temple of the Spirit, she is the first human being who unconditionally allowed these Three to do for our race what they had intended "before ever the world was made" (*Ep* 1:4) - namely, that we should share in their own life, their holiness, and their supreme joy. "Father," Jesus prayed, "I desire that they also, whom thou hast given me, may be with me where I am, to behold my glory" (*Jn* 17:24). True of all of us, this is uniquely true of the one whom it pleases us to call "Our Blessed Lady".

Pope Francis has reminded us that we arrive at being "where Christ is", by sharing in his death and resurrection. Quarton rightly positions the cross as the link between heaven and earth, the "keyhole" of the door through which we must chose or refuse to pass. "No one comes to the Father except through me," says Christ, and he does not lie (*Jn* 14:6).

Entering through the door which is Christ himself, we discover that we do so as members of a vast people coming from all corners of the world and from every walk of life. Pope Francis has underlined how "inclusive" this people is and must be. The American writer, Flannery O'Connor, describes it as being a case of "Here comes everyone!" This is the Church - in heaven, on earth and in purgatory (cf. *CCC* 1030-1032). But we are not gathered into some amorphous mass, we are not assumed into some unconscious *nirvana*, nothingness. We were not created as persons in order to end up as clouds! We can identify and name many of the angels and saints represented by the artist here; and we will recognise each other when, as St Thomas More put it, we meet "merrily in Heaven", if each has but obeyed God in the depth of his or her conscience.

Quarton gives a wonderful depiction of the mystery of communion which Pope Francis has opened up for us anew, and to which we are called "to bear radiant witness". We do so, in the words of the hymn, by "service, ardent and generous faith, justice and love of the poor" - all of which is the hallmark of the lives of the saints we see represented in such splendid colour! But, by the hue of the two cloaks which envelop her and the detail of the pattern around her neck and her crown, we note that Mary shares to a unique degree in the love that binds the Blessed Three in One. From there, she looks out towards us. As our mother she presents our needs to the Lord, so that that the joy of the Gospel may truly "reach to the ends of the earth, illuminating even the fringes of our world".

It is this mystery of communion which is brought about and celebrated in every Mass, where matter is transformed into Christ's Body and Blood, and we "become what we eat", as St Augustine put it. And so it shall be, throughout all ages, "until God be all in all" (*1 Co* 15:28). Then, together with Mary, all the angels and the saints, our hearts will ring out with true and eternal joy, the joy of our Maker! (cf. *CCC* 1024). Amen.

Canticles for Prayer

The Benedictus

Blessed be the Lord, the God of Israel!
He has visited his people and redeemed them.
He has raised up for us a mighty saviour
in the house of David his servant,
as he promised by the lips of holy men,
those who were his prophets from of old.
A saviour who would free us from our foes,
from the hands of all who hate us.
So his love for our fathers is fulfilled
and his holy covenant remembered.
He swore to Abraham our father to grant us,
that free from fear, and saved from the hands
  of our foes,
we might serve him in holiness and justice
all the days of our life in his presence.
As for you, little child,
you shall be called a prophet of God, the Most High.
You shall go ahead of the Lord
to prepare his ways before him.
To make known to his people their salvation

through forgiveness of all their sins,
the loving-kindness of the heart of our God
who visits us like the dawn from on high.
He will give light to those in darkness,
those who dwell in the shadow of death,
and guide us into the way of peace.

Magnificat

My soul glorifies the Lord,
my spirit rejoices in God, my Saviour.
He looks on his servant in her lowliness;
henceforth all ages will call me blessed.
The Almighty works marvels for me.
Holy his name!
His mercy is from age to age,
on those who fear him.
He puts forth his arm in strength
and scatters the proudhearted.
He casts the mighty from their thrones
and raises the lowly.
He fills the starving with good things,
sends the rich away empty.
He protects Israel, his servant,
remembering his mercy,
the mercy promised to our fathers,
to Abraham and his sons for ever.

Reading plans

50 Day Reading Plan for *Evangelii Gaudium*
Time allowance: 15 minutes per day
Numbers refer to paragraphs

Day 1	1-5	Day 26	154-159
Day 2	6-13	Day 27	160-168
Day 3	14-18	Day 28	169-175
Day 4	19-24	Day 29	176-179
Day 5	25-29	Day 30	180-185
Day 6	30-33	Day 31	186-192
Day 7	34-39	Day 32	193-196
Day 8	40-45	Day 33	197-201
Day 9	46-49	Day 34	202-208
Day 10	50-56	Day 35	209-216
Day 11	57-63	Day 36	217-221
Day 12	64-70	Day 37	222-225
Day 13	71-75	Day 38	226-230
Day 14	76-80	Day 39	231-233
Day 15	81-86	Day 40	234-237
Day 16	87-92	Day 41	238-241
Day 17	93-101	Day 42	242-246
Day 18	102-109	Day 43	247-254
Day 19	110-114	Day 44	255-258
Day 20	115-121	Day 45	259-263
Day 21	122-129	Day 46	264-267
Day 22	130-134	Day 47	268-274
Day 23	135-141	Day 48	275-280
Day 24	142-148	Day 49	281-283
Day 25	149-153	Day 50	284-288

1 Month Reading Plan for *Evangelii Gaudium*
Time allowance: 25 minutes per day
Numbers refer to paragraphs

Day 1	1-8	Day 16	149-155
Day 2	9-18	Day 17	156-168
Day 3	19-29	Day 18	169-175
Day 4	30-39	Day 19	176-185
Day 5	40-49	Day 20	186-196
Day 6	50-60	Day 21	197-208
Day 7	61-70	Day 22	209-216
Day 8	71-80	Day 23	217-225
Day 9	81-92	Day 24	226-233
Day 10	93-101	Day 25	234-241
Day 11	102-109	Day 26	242-249
Day 12	110-118	Day 27	250-258
Day 13	119-129	Day 28	259-267
Day 14	130-138	Day 29	268-280
Day 15	139-148	Day 30	281-288

2 Week Reading Plan for *Evangelii Gaudium*
Time allowance: 45 minutes per day
Numbers refer to paragraphs

Day 1	1-18	Day 8	145-159
Day 2	19-39	Day 9	160-175
Day 3	40-60	Day 10	176-201
Day 4	61-80	Day 11	202-221
Day 5	81-101	Day 12	222-237
Day 6	102-121	Day 13	238-258
Day 7	122-144	Day 14	259-288

Endnotes

[1] *Annunciation*, by Henry Ossawa Tanner (1859-1937); an Afro-American artist (Philadelphia Museum of Art, used here with permission).

[2] Pronounced *ee-van-gai-lee gow-dee-um*. The Latin title is always the opening two words of papal documents, which are very carefully chosen to sum up the theme of the work.

[3] Benedict XVI, *Homily at the Mass for the Inauguration of his Pontificate*, 24th April 2005.

[4] Popes write their documents with numbered paragraphs for ease of reference. You will find that the *Catechism of the Catholic Church* and the *Documents of the Second Vatican Council* are written in the same way.

[5] In this Apostolic Exhortation, Pope Francis notes that it is upon the basis of this constant teaching of the Church that his appeal is being made. He refers us, for example, to the Church's documents on catechesis - the transmission of the faith (no. 163) - and recommends to us the *Compendium of the Social Doctrine of the Church* (no. 184).

[6] This word is derived from the Latin, *beatus*.

[7] Vatican II produced four key documents, known as Constitutions: *Sacrosanctum Concilium* (on the Liturgy); *Dei Verbum* (on Sacred Scripture and Tradition); *Gaudium et Spes* (on the Church in the Modern World); and *Lumen Gentium* (on the Mystery of Christ and the Church).

[8] Vatican Council II, Lumen Gentium 11.

[9] Pope Benedict XVI, 'The Priest and Pastoral Ministry in a Digital World: New Media at the Service of the Word', 44th World Communications Day, January 24, 2010. *Agora* is a Greek word meaning 'gathering place'. The idea is that social networks are a new, virtual, kind of public 'gathering place'.

[10] Romance VIII, in *Collected Works of John of the Cross* (trans E. Allison Peers) (Kessinger Publishing, 2010)

[11] Chesterton, G.K., 'Mary and the Convert', *The Well and the Shallows* (Aziloth Books, 2012) pp.96-98

[12] Quarton, Enguerrand(1410-1466), *The Assumption and Crowning of Our Lady* (Villeneuve-les-Avignon). Used here with permission.